Planet

William B. Rice

Consultant

JoBea Holt, Ph.D.
The Climate Project
Nashville, Tennessee

Publishing Credits

Dona Herweck Rice, *Editor-in-Chief*; Lee Aucoin, *Creative Director*; Don Tran, *Print Production Manager*; Timothy J. Bradley, *Illustration Manager*; Chris McIntyre, *Editorial Director*; James Anderson, *Associate Editor*; Jamey Acosta, *Associate Editor*; Jane Gould, *Editor*; Peter Balaskas, *Editorial Administrator*; Neri Garcia, *Senior Designer*; Stephanie Reid, *Photo Editor*; Rachelle Cracchiolo, M.S.Ed., *Publisher*

Image Credits

cover L. Cook/Photo Researchers, Inc.; p.1 L. Cook/Photo Researchers, Inc.; p.5 Jurgen Ziewe/Shutterstock; p.6 Sebastian Kaulitzki/Shutterstock; p.7 NASA; p.8 magaliB/iStockphoto; p.10-11 Stephanie Reid; p.12-13 Andrea Danti/Shutterstock; p.14 Craig Wactor/Shutterstock; p.15 bicubic/Shutterstock; p.16 NASA p.17 NASA; p.18 Jaan-Martin Juusmann/Shutterstock; p.19 (top) Jordan James Munyon Martin/Shutterstock, (bottom) NASA; p.20 (top) Plutonius 3d/Shutterstock, (bottom) NASA; p.21 (top) peresanz/Shutterstock, (bottom) July Flower/Shutterstock; p.22 (left) Stephen Girimont/Shutterstock, (right) NASA; p.23 (left) NASA, (right) Sabino Parente/Shutterstock; p.24 (top) NASA, (bottom) bluecrayola/Shutterstock; p.25 (top) NASA, (bottom) Michael Taylor/Shutterstock; p.26 Dagadu/Dreamstime; p.27 Alex Staroseltsev/Shutterstock; p.28 Rocket400 Studio/Shutterstock; p.29 Karen Lowe; p.32 McMullan Co./Newscom

Teacher Created Materials

5301 Oceanus Drive
Huntington Beach, CA 92649-1030
http://www.tcmpub.com

ISBN 978-1-4333-1422-3
©2011 Teacher Created Materials, Inc.
Reprinted 2012

Table of Contents

The Solar System

Space is a big place. It has **trillions** of stars and planets! Our sun is just one of those stars. Eight planets move around our sun.

The planets orbit the sun. To **orbit** means to move around something.

The sun and its planets are called the **solar system**.

sun

We live on one of the planets. Our planet is Earth. Earth is the third planet from the sun.

sun

Earth

Earth

Mercury is the first planet. It is close to the sun. Neptune is the eighth planet. It is very far away.

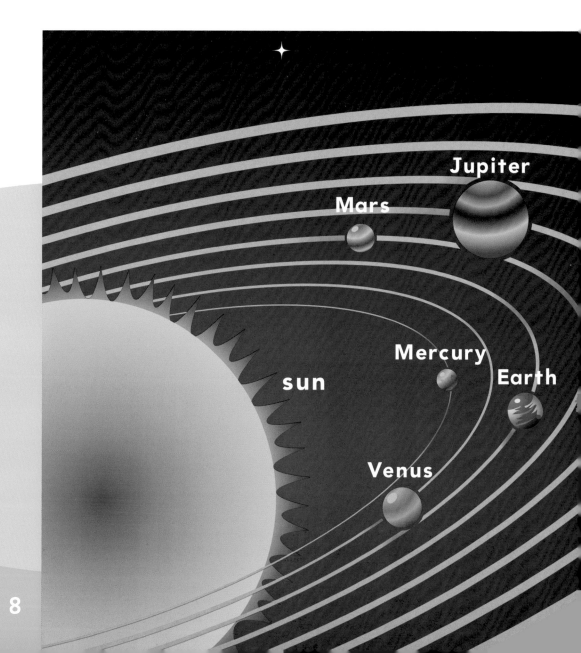

A Long Year

Neptune is so far away that it takes 165 Earth years to go around the sun just one time!

Neptune

Saturn

Uranus

Each planet moves in its own **orbit**, or path.

All planets move the same way around the sun. They move counterclockwise. Each planet also spins as it moves.

moon

Earth

sun

clockwise

counterclockwise

The Planets

Each planet is its own size. Mercury is small. Two and one half Mercurys could fit inside Earth. Jupiter is big. About 1,300 Earths could fit inside Jupiter!

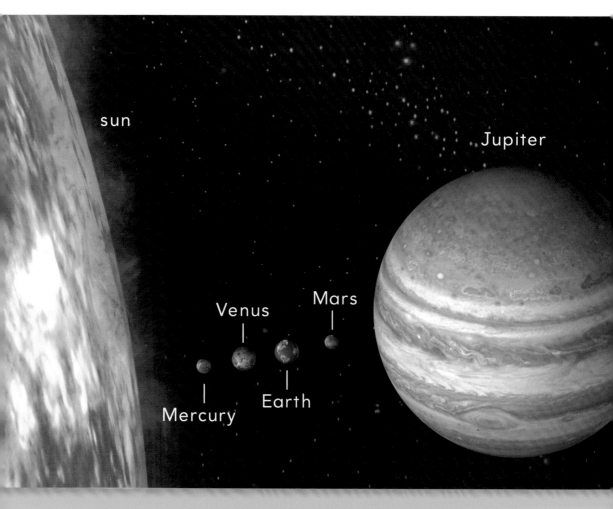

sun

Jupiter

Venus

Mars

Mercury

Earth

Mercury is about 36 million miles from the sun. Earth is about 93 million miles from the sun.

Saturn

Uranus

Neptune

The sun is really big! It is bigger than all the planets. Imagine that the solar system was the same as 100 pennies. Then, the sun would be the same as 98 of those pennies. Everything else in the solar system would be just the 2 pennies that are left!

Each planet is made in its own way.
Some planets are hard and rocky. They are
made of rock and **metal**.

Mercury, Venus,
Earth, and Mars
are the rocky
planets.

the surface of Mars

Mars

Some planets are made mainly of **gas**.
They are like big, heavy rain clouds.

Jupiter

Jupiter, Saturn, Uranus, and Neptune are the gas planets.

Neptune

Saturn

Mercury looks like Earth's moon. It has big holes called **craters**. Venus is about the same size as Earth. It is easy to spot Venus in the night sky.

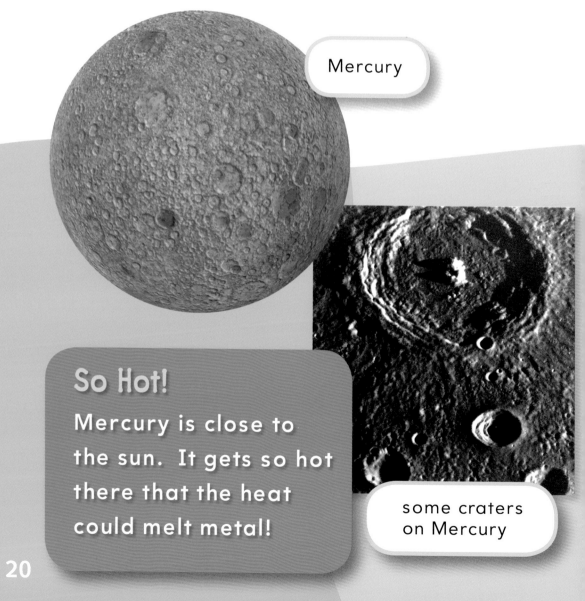

Mercury

So Hot!

Mercury is close to the sun. It gets so hot there that the heat could melt metal!

some craters on Mercury

Venus

Earth's
moon

Venus

Earth is our planet. It is the best planet for life. Mars is called the red planet. That is because the soil on Mars is red. Jupiter is the biggest planet. It is also a planet that spins very fast!

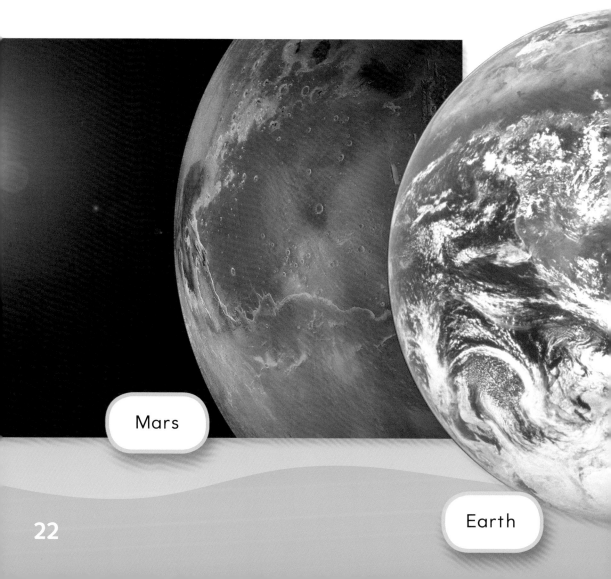

Mars

Earth

Jupiter

There are many rings around Saturn. The rings are made of rock and ice. Winter on Uranus lasts for 21 years! Summer lasts for 21 years, too. Neptune has lots of big winds. Some storms on Neptune are as big as Earth itself!

a close-up look at the rings of Saturn

Saturn

Neptune

storm

Uranus

We Are Here!

The solar system is a big place. Earth is just a small part of it. But it is an important part! The solar system would not be the same without it.

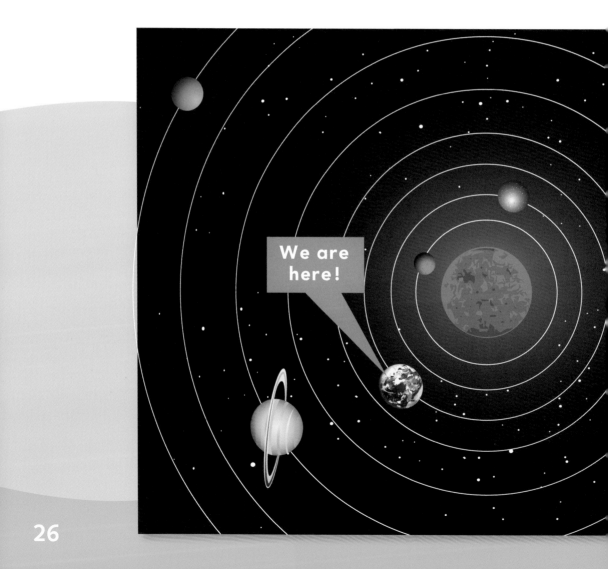

Science Lab: Day and Night

Do this activity to learn about day and night.

Materials:

- Styrofoam ball
- pushpin
- stick or pencil
- flashlight

Procedure:

❶ Place the ball on the end of the stick or pencil. The ball is a planet.

❷ Stick the pushpin somewhere into the ball. The pin is you on the planet.

❸ Hold the stick in your left hand.

❹ Turn on the flashlight. Hold it in your right hand. The flashlight is the sun.

❺ Point the light (sun) at the ball (planet).

❻ Turn the stick or pencil slowly. This will make the planet spin.

❼ Watch the planet. The part in the light is day. The part in the dark is night. If you are the pin, are you in day or night?

❽ Real World: Is it day or night for you right now in the real world? Where is the sun compared to where you are?

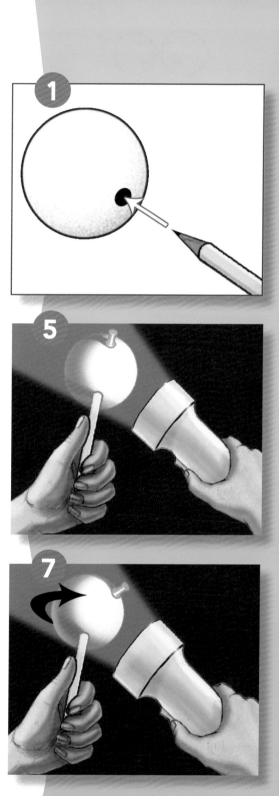

Glossary

craters—large holes or dents

gas—a state of matter that is not solid or liquid

metal—a solid substance like gold, silver, and copper

orbit—to move around something in a circle or oval shape

planetarium—a building or room that uses lights, projectors, and models to show what space is like

solar system—the sun and everything that moves around it

trillion—a million millions; 1,000,000,000,000

Index

A Scientist Today

Neil deGrasse Tyson is a scientist who studies space. He runs an important **planetarium**. He also talks about planets and space on television shows. Neil wants everyone to learn about space.